SMERALDO

'THE SINCERITY I COULD NOT DELIVER'

SEHAJPREET KAUR

Crazy stuff happens around me, And yet being stable seems the most challenging part...

Contents

Contents

Contents

Preface

Sometimes conveying messages very honestly is hard. Very hard. I know.

I've had both Ranging as well as Racing emotions.

Ranging; I never knew people I admired could be hated by my heart. Those peers I thought were a blessing to have around turned into curses. After a dark storm passes, there's only one warrior that stands strong. One warrior with a supporting sword. As the dark clouds of sorrow emerge everyone thinks of themselves as a fighter, but when the clouds pass, they take it all along. However, rain is always scary until you have an umbrella.

Racing; Emotions can be extreme. They may cause you to respect yourself as a queen but at the same time to drown yourself as some worthless belonging. A human's internal feelings can be dangerous, and they are dangerous. All have their own groups, their own 'Buddies' but when they need something all those groups are suddenly non-existent, and it is as if, they can only and only see me. When they need something, when they want to fulfill their purpose, I am everyone's target. But every dog is dangerous only until you learn to tame one.

Through the process of completing this book, I had to feel all sorts of emotions to bring this poetry to life. I had to train my mind to go through different attributes of life. To observe around me. And that was when I realized - Life is an ocean, which may be a pleasant ride if you have a boat but a deadly experience if you don't.

So all I have to do is to have something to protect me from my hardships.

To provide my mind with a shield.

Sounds like a piece of cake, but trust me, IT IS A PIECE OF CAKE, just make it your favorite flavor, and it will be a piece of cake.

Trust me.

Smeraldo, as the title suggests means, the sincerity one couldn't deliver. In this book, I have discussed various themes through poems, the themes which are parts of life and where humans struggle to express their true beliefs.

AMOR, VITA, ADULSCENS, FEMINA & NATURA. Love, Life, Youth, Women, and Nature.

As for love, whether be parent love, sibling love, or the 'LOVE' love, we always do struggle in conveying our very honest feelings. 'Oh! it's too cheesy' we say when expressing love to our parents, 'I am scared' when doing so to our lovers. Every now and then we struggle.

The same goes for life, youth, women, and for nature.

Life is a scary ride; But those who understand it, enjoy it; the others scream in fear.

Acknowledgements

I, me and myself.

Amor

Love

1. Permitted Love?

A tree once said to another
"Oh! I'm in love with you"
She said, "No! It can't happen"
He said, "Why? Nature can fall in love too."

2. Love?

Mother! Oh! Mother
Asked the little girl
What is that feeling?
They all call love.
Oh! My sweetheart
Said the mother to her
Just the way you say my name
Is truly called love.

3. I Wish I......

I wish I had a superpower,
Not to Vanish, Not to fly,
But to make my dreams,
Come to life.
Because in my dreams,
You are actually mine,
And I stare at you,
As you shine.

4. Lust isn't Love?

They say lust isn't love,
How could you deduce,
Juice whether apple or mango,
Still remains a juice.
Whether sweet or sour,
A lemon still has seeds,
Love whether love or lust,
Still has the pure deeds.

5. I Come To You, Always....

In the nights dark and deep,
Nights when everyone's asleep,
Everyone's asleep so I slowly creep,
Creep towards you to take a peep.
And you sit there,
Looking here,
Right where,
I sit unaware.
And then you look at me,
And I look at you to see,
To see you staring back at me,
Back at me, you look with glee,
With glee, you tell me that you love me.

6. You'll Know It

You know that it's happened,
When you cannot take your eyes,
Off of that person,
You'll do anything to look at twice.

7. Only for Once

I wish I could,
Only for once,
Just have the fortune to,
Hold your hand.

8. The Touch of ______

When I held her hand,
For the very first time,
I knew it was her,
i knew she was mine.
Wrapped in her arms,
I felt out of danger,
Her touch so soft,
The touch of my mother.

9. A serenade of Love

Your touch,
It made me feel like a queen,
It made me so,
I could not sleep.
If I'm being honest,
It felt so sweet,
But also, as hot as,
Hell's feet.

10. You and Me

You came to me,
To me through those dreams,
It made an impact,
An impact that could be seen.
They linked us together,
Together we were called,
When i was sad it was you,
And for you, I was informed.
I knew it then,
Knew that it would last forever,
Lasting past lives and deaths,
Lives and deaths we'll be together.

11. Me

Me?
Are you talking about me?
Do I deserve this happiness?
Why am I so restless?
So privileged to be,
I hope this isn't a dream,
Cuz if it's a dreamy ride,
It's gonna be one of a kind.
Getting used to this,
Is gonna be tough,
To be with you,
Is gonna be sweet yet rough.
Oh you,
You gave me life,
Or I would've died,
In the bathroom that night.
Promise me
Promise me you won't leave
I need you next to me
Close to you, I need to be.
Why me?
Why did you choose me?
Why me of all?
Why catch me when I fall?

Thank you,
For blessing me like this,
With the reality of my,
Scripted dream.
Can I see you once,
May I talk to you,
Oh let me touch you, please,
I beg on my knees.
Did I know you all along?
Those feelings seemed all a joke,
Until I realized,
This life of mine is a prize,
The prize that is you,
Standing mine so true.

12. Tragic Love

A tree once fell in love,
With one of its flowers,
They would dance and sway together,
In the beautiful showers.
One day a little girl,
So innocent and sweet,
Plucked the little flower,
As she walked away on her feet.
She admired the little beauty,
With sparkles in her eyes,
Whereas the tree and the flower,
Bid their last goodbyes.

13. Almost

I kept thinking of,
When we almost held hands,
When you almost told me,
What you felt.
When we almost got drenched in rain,
When we almost fell from a pine,
And I kept thinking of the time,
Of the time you were almost mine.

14. A Breeze Like You...

Your warm touch,
Fills my empty vessel,
When you held my hand,
It felt so special.
When it rained,
You came along the breeze,
And slid through the window,
Into my room with ease.

15. A Thread with a Knot

Let's say we moved on,
From the sorrow that we suffered,
It still wouldn't have ended well,
We would still have stuttered.
The hesitation said it all,
It was meant to end short,
No yes-es and no no-s,
When our thread got a knot.

Vita

Life

16. Comfort

Sometimes it's those words,
sometimes a mere effort,
Sometimes it's a hug,
That is enough to provide comfort.

17. Words

Words create ripples,
Ripples that travel far,
Ripples that never return,
Ripples that tear us apart.
Those words once spoken,
May create rage,
Thay may create love,
May vreate a new page.

18. Just Another Day...

A world I cherished,
Came to an end,
The sweet blue dreams,
Were black to portend.
Too soon to smile,
Too late to cry,
My heart felt cold,
And eyes were dry.
The feeling dissappeared during day,
Came back rushing at night,
As tears rolled down,
When i lay there alright.
Was it me who overthought ,
Or were the events overwhelming,
That threw me down so hard,
And so getting back up was challenging.
I wish i could scream,
So you could hear,
So you could know,
What all i fear.
Honestly it hurts me,
Hurts me deep inside,
That you never try to ask,
What's actually on my mind.

19. Lies

They made me believe,
Believe in their flowers,
The flowers that looked tempting,
The flowers that left scars.
A lighthouse,
Which lit up at dark nights,
But when I went in,
It was lonely and full of fright.
I sat alone,
Sat alone as I sighed,
Still thinking about,
How I believed your lies.

20. I Smile

Just because I smile in front of you,
You take me for granted,
But when I'm alone,
You never knew how long my tears lasted.
And because I love to make people happy,
That doesn't mean I'm happy myself,
Slits on my arm and my neck I stranded,
When my patience fell off the shelf.
Just let me be,
One day I know I'll die,
So why can't today be,
The day I don't have to try.
When you lose me you'll know my worth,
You'll know when I slip away from your grasp,
You'll know how big a mess my life had been,
And then you'll regret you never asked.

21. No One

Who shall I share my sadness with,
With whom shall I share my sorrow,
All of them turn their backs at me,
All of them put it to tomorrow.
And yet again I go to see,
What will possibly happen to me,
They tell me it's enough when I cry,
They tell me we'll be done if I try.
So in the end I'm all alone,
I walked down the street as the moon shone,
It rained and then it poured,
And in the end, I was all alone.

22. Dreams

They say, "Dreams are illusions,
They don't mean a thing.
You'll eventually forget them,
When you wake up in the morning."
But, They hide a deeper meaning,
They tell stories,
They tell me about you,
And you about me.
We don't need to remember a thing,
It just stays in the heart,
We think about it and amile,
We think about it and cry.
They come like wind,
But stay like rain,
As they pour for a while,
And then go away.
I wish one such dream,
About me came to you,
And I wait patiently,
In hoped you know about me too.

23. What Do I Want?

Deep in my thoughts,
As I wander alone,
I realize what I want the most,
Is for my pain to be known.

24. What Did I Mean To You?

You took your chance,
Pushed me aside,
Forgot all the promises,
You said by which you'd abide.
I was nothing to you,
Nothing at all,
From the very beginning,
You yourself were the one you wanted it for.

25. Hurts

I think words hurt deeper,
Than the sharpest knives cut.
I think it hurts being slammed in the face,
Than all the doors being shut.
And yet I thought that she was lying,
When she said that it hurt.

Adulescens

Youth

26. Tastes Like….

The soup tastes like happiness
Tea tastes like comfort
These days every food I eat
Tastes like something or the other.
Coffee tastes like action
It tastes like hero spirit
Yet wine tastes so calm
It tastes like a sweet secret.

27. Blue Sand and Red Crabs

I'd say it was a different world,
A different place,
Yet to be discovered.
Just like a fairyland,
As the blue sand blew,
It took my breath away,
When the red crabs flew.
Around my body,
The wind whirled,
And from a distance,
A butterfly unfurled.
It flew to me,
With a bright gleam,
And whispered to me,
Welcome to your dream.

28. The Chitter Chatter

Paper balls,
Around the room,
the chitter chatter,
Will soon resume.
The teacher leaves,
The sounds boom,
The chitter chatter,
In my classroom.

29. Those Times...

Those times,
When one is carefree,
When one is selfless,
When one grows like a tree.
Those times they,
Influence what you become,
Influence your present and future,
Influence your next big turn.

30. Be With Me

I met you,
In those winters cold,
In times I had no one,
To see how it unfolds.
I had been hurt before,
It was new to see,
To be around someone,
Who was so caring towards me.
Though I still have trust issues,
Though I don't know how it will end,
But I promise let's last forever,
Be till death my Best Friend.

31. Happiness

Just because I smile in front of you,
You take me for granted,
But when I'm alone,
You never knew how long my tears lasted.
And because I love to make people happy,
Doesn't mean I'm happy myself,
Slits on my arm and my neck I stranded,
When my patience fell off the shelf.
Just let me be,
One day I know I'll die,
So why can't today be,
The day I don't have to try.
When you lose me you'll know my worth,
You'll know when I slip away from your grasp,
You'll know how big a mess my life had been,
And then you'll regret you never asked.

32. Salt and Sugar

Sweet is sugar,
Salt too much can be bitter,
But salt reflects light,
It fools us together.
If he seems to shine,
If being with him adds flavor to you,
He may be sugar,
But his shining could make him salt too.

33. My Best Friend

When you're with me,
It's all fine,
We stick together,
Partners in crime.
Now that you're gone,
They treat me as if,
I am a virus,
Who would make them stiff.

34. Bilbury is Deaf

Bilbury is deaf,
He can't hear what you say,
He walks down the lane,
Watching the trees sway.
I once stopped by,
And interpreted, "Why do you walk out?"
He responded, "The green is enough,
To tell me all about."

35. It Didn't Mean That......

And just because,
I opened up to you,
My open wound,
Didn't mean,
That I trusted you.

36. Exam

Heart racing, Skin sweating,
Notebooks in hand ready to cram,
Look around a tense vibe,
On the day of the exam.

Femina

Woman

37. I Know of a Warrior

I know of a warrior,
Who's brave and hearty,
I know of a warrior,
Who's elegant and classy.
I know of a warrior,
I know of a woman,
I know of a warrior,
I know of her.

38. When She Falls

When a woman,
Falls to her knees,
She doesn't fall alone,
Falls along a forest of trees.

39. Mother

Mother Earth, Mother Nature,
We say.
Then where's the respect,
To our mother we should pay?

40. Tell me how you do it

Tell me how you do it,
As you stand apart,
While you stare at me,
With silent eyes and a cold heart.
Tell me how you do it,
When you tell lies,
So easily with a smile,
As your inner honesty dies.
Tell me how you do it,
As you manage to escape,
From all the sins that you committed,
On your way to my place.

41. A Woman

I am a woman,
Delicate as a flower,
But also a monster,
With a lot of power.
I could help you,
I could guide you and be kind,
But i could also,
Be rude like no one you'd find.

42. Treasure. Men or women?

They say, "A woman is a treasure,
She could make you feel under the weather."
But excuse me for a while,
Why only women when men's also got the treasure pile.

Natura

Nature

43. A Flower

They think I am beautiful,
Hence I am plucked,
Humans are wierd creatures,
They hurt the ones they love.

44. Just Like

You came to me,
Like rain pours.
And went away,
Like water flows.

45. Daisy

A tinge of yellow for innocence,
white like a pure lady,
A symbol of true love,
A flower of daisy.

46. Alone Little Bunny

I sit in my tiny hole,
Well under the ground,
Not too deep,
It's shallow and sound.
It's raining outisde,
The soil's getting wet,
my fur can feel it,
Staying away from my family now feels like regret.

47. Comfort For Me

Is it the sky that calls,
When my hopeless heart falls,
Are those the clouds,
Who smile at me out loud,
Is it the moon,
That brings me back in tune,
Are those the stars,
Who erase my scars.

48. A Dreamy Sight

In a meadow,
I saw a few,
Butterflies with their,
Dresses soaked in dew.

49. The Willow Tree

The willow tree,
That stands by,
The path to my house,
Through the grassy ally.
The willow tree,
That stands strong,
When it rains,
For so long.
The willow tree,
That stands proud,
In the scorching sun,
When there're no clouds.
The willow tree,
It looks at me,
With all the love,
That one could see.

50. Who Is It?

Is it the sky that calls,
When my hopeless heart falls,
Are those the clouds,
Who smile at me out loud,
Is it the moon,
That brings me back in tune,
Are those the stars,
Who erase my scars.

Why Did I Write This Book?

Poetry I knew was always a tool that'd help people engage in the spirit of self love. Loving and respecting oneself is tough to achieve but beautiful to live through.

People often care for others more than they do for themselves, ignoring oneself is the biggest mistake we are making as the youth of today's generation. My actual aim for writing this book was to make sure I in some way am able to help people recognise their true feelings and express it through poetry.

Inspiration

Seeing a picture of people we all know, but hate, you might wanna throw this book away right now, but trust me, once you read the true inspiration behind this book, you'll want to read it further. I'm not telling you to like these 7 boys, I'm just giving honest credit to the ones who helped me find an inspiration for one the best books I ever wrote.

The name of the book 'Smeraldo', which translates to 'Sincerity that could not be delivered', comes from the very famous band - BTS. The flower- Smeraldo, was used as a symbol in their albumn 'Love Yourself- Her'.

The flower was introduced to the world on august 9, 2017, by one of the members. Even though BTS introduced this flower to the world, the legend of this flower travels far back.

[The flower is known to have originally bloomed in "La Citta Di Smeraldo". A flourishing city which, supposedly, was located in Northern Italy, during medieval times, but was abandoned after the black death.

According to a map which has surfaced in recent times, "La Citta Di Smeraldo" is estimated to have been located in northern Italy which is now a rural village.

The smeraldo flower is quite symbolical.

It represents an entangled love story surrounding the smeraldo which is estimated to have taken place around the 15th-16th centuries in the city of "La Citta di smeraldo".

According to various sources, the story supposedly has a tragic ending filled with yearning, sadness and sincerity that could not be delivered.

According to the story, there once lived a man. He lived in a secluded castle in La Citta di smeraldo.

There is not much information about the man except that he was the 'love child' of the duke of Florence who fell in love with a poor gardener's daughter. She passed away at childbirth due to excessive bleeding leaving the man alone in the world.

Being a child born out of wedlock, he was the source of misery to the wife and children of the duke, who tried to kill the poor boy. As a result, the duke sent him to a place further away.

There were many rumors, but none was revealed.

It is said the man alone hid in solitude at the old castle and wore a mask because he was very 'ugly'. Probably because of all the hatred and jealousy he received as he lived, he didn't open his heart to anyone. When anyone tried to approach him, he would hide away in anger and distrust.

He shut himself from the world. Both his body and his heart.

His only joy was to grow flowers in his garden.

It made him happy and peaceful.

But things took a beautiful turn. A turn which would be a moment of beauty within the memories at the corner of his head.

A turn that would leave a sorrowful scar his heart forever and bring in tears to his eyes.

Fate was playing on him.

One day, a girl appeared in front of him near the vicinity of his castle. She was in ragged clothes. As he watched, the girl picked up the heels of the garden fence, climbed over it, and stole some flowers.

The man was mad as a hornet at first. He was mad at her for stealing his precious flowers. He spent his whole night guarding the flowers. But in his brief moment of sleep, the girl picked up some flowers and ran away. Several nights continued to pass like that until the man pretended to be asleep and watched the girl go. He was curious.

Who was she? Why does she steal my blooming pretty flowers every night?

Without realizing it, the man waited for the girl and followed her one night. He disguised himself with a cloak and followed her.

After following her to a village, he realized why she stole flowers in his garden every night.

He found out that the girl sells these flowers because she is very poor and has no other way to provide a living for herself.

He felt very bad for her. Guilt filled him up.

The man wanted to help the girl. He wanted to teach her every method of growing flowers he knew. He wanted to teach her how to grow beautiful flowers.

He was slowly falling in love with her.

The man started growing many flowers for her and made sure they were of the best quality.

He wanted to show up in front of her. Tell her of his feelings towards her. But, he knew he could not show up in front of her.

She would be scared of him.

He must hide. Because he was ugly. She would not love his ugly appearance.

So he never got the courage to confront her

At the end, the only thing he could do was to grow and take care of the flowers so that she would keep coming to his garden.

With time, he decided to himself that he would grow the most expensive flower(the Smeraldo)for her to sell. That was the only way he would unveil his sincerity to her.

He locked himself in the castle.

After many attempts, he succeeded in making the flower. The flower was lovely. It was something that never existed in the world. Afterward, he filled his garden with the flower and waited till nightfall for the girl to return.

He waited and waited for the girl to come back to the garden to steal the flower. But the girl did not return. She was nowhere to be seen.No matter how much he waited, the girl wouldn't return to his garden.

It made him anxious. He later visited the village he followed her to.

Unfortunately, he found out that the girl had died.]

(-source: indrachapa.medium.com

https://indrachapa.medium.com/legend-of-the-smeraldo-flower-d0e689b167af#:~:text=It's%20said%20smeraldo(flower)

stands,abandoned%20after%20the%20black%20death.)

And so the flower translates to 'The truth that couldn't be told'.

Why Did I Pick This Inspiration?

Through the poetry in this book, I've tried to portray emotions that humans usually leave unattended and the ones which are usually ignored.

In this cycle of life, we are all very busy with our daily lives, and so we forget what adds to the real meaning of this role we are playing.

The poetry collection here aims to help ease one's emotions and help them understand themselves better. To be able to tell oneself how we feel is the biggest achievement. Understanding oneself is a challenge only very few may be able to overcome.

www.ingramcontent.com/pod-product-compliance
Ingram Content Group UK Ltd.
Pitfield, Milton Keynes, MK11 3LW, UK
UKHW042012190726
13854UKWH00005B/2262